The Art of Sugarcraft

LACE AND FILIGREE

The Art of Sugarcraft

LACE AND FILIGREE

NICHOLAS LODGE

Foreword Jenny Campbell
Series Editor Joyce Becker
Photography Graham Tann

MEREHURST PRESS
LONDON

Published 1987 by Merehurst Press
5 Great James Street
London WC1N 3DA

ISBN 0 948075 56 2

Designed by Carole Perks
Editorial Assistant Suzanne Ellis
Typeset by Filmset
Colour separation by Fotographics Ltd, London-Hong Kong
Printed by New Interlitho S.p.A., Milan

ACKNOWLEDGEMENTS
I dedicate this book to my grandparents, for their love and support, and to all my overseas cake decorating friends in Australia, Africa and the Far East.

Thanks to Lucy, Graham and Stewart for their help.

The Publishers would like to thank the following for their help and advice:
C.E.P. Chocolate & Sugar Moulds, 7 Durrington Road,
    Bournemouth BH7 6PU
Elizabeth David Ltd, 46 Bourne Street, London SW1W 8JD and at
    Covent Garden Kitchen Supplies, 3 North Row, The Market,
    Covent Garden, London WC2
B.R. Mathews & Son, 12 Gipsy Hill, Upper Norwood,
    London SE19 1NN
Guy Paul and Company Limited, Unit B4, A1 Industrial Park,
    Little End Road, Eton Scoton, Cambridgeshire, PE19 3JH
John F. Renshaw & Company Limited, Locks Lane, Mitcham,
    Surrey CR4 2XE
Anne Smith
Antique lace kindly supplied by Joyce Becker, Jill Twomey and
Suzanne Ellis
Cross-stitch plaque design from *Favorite Charted Designs* by
Anne Orr, copyright Dover Publications, Inc., New York
Trellis cradle based on an original design by Mary Tipton, St. Ives,
Cornwall

Companion volumes:
The Art of Sugarcraft — **MARZIPAN**
The Art of Sugarcraft — **CHOCOLATE**
The Art of Sugarcraft — **PIPING**
The Art of Sugarcraft — **SUGAR FLOWERS**
The Art of Sugarcraft — **SUGARPASTE**
The Art of Sugarcraft — **ROYAL ICING**
The Art of Sugarcraft — **PASTILLAGE AND SUGAR MOULDING**

CONTENTS

FOREWORD

This is an excellent book which I feel will be unequalled in its field. I have known Nick since 1978 when we were both attending the National Bakery School. Immediately he impressed me with his exceptional talent, versatility and imagination, together with speed, skill and dexterity.

Over the past nine years, during which time he has been employed as a cake designer and lecturer on the subject, I have seen his work enhanced by his wider interests in art, floristry and natural history. This attention to detail is shown in the lace inserts taken from patterns of antique lace and the lace and filigree butterflies and flowers in this lovely book.

Nick teaches at classes held at my shop and therefore I have been able to witness the enthusiasm he has created in the students. I know the pleasure and help to be gained from the precise instructions and beautiful illustrations in this book will give inspiration to all sugar artists.

JENNY CAMPBELL
Owner, B.R. Mathews, Sugarcraft specialist shop.

NICHOLAS LODGE

Nicholas Lodge is one of the brightest lights in the young generation of sugarcraft artists. Although still in his early twenties, he already has an impressive collection of awards for his outstanding skills in the field of cake decoration.

Nicholas studied cake decoration at the National Bakery School, London, where he was awarded the prize for the best decoration student in his final year. He then worked in a bakery to gain practical experience before joining one of Britain's leading commercial cake decorating firms. As principal designer, Nicholas was responsible for producing cakes commissioned from leading stores and hotels. He also taught Australian and South African icing techniques.

He has taught sugarcraft to students at all levels, as well as demonstrating cake decorating and chocolate work in shops and department stores all over the UK. In addition, he has taught cake decorating in Singapore, Malaysia, Indonesia, Japan, and southern Africa.

In 1986, Nicholas wrote *Sugar Flowers* and co-authored *Chocolate* in THE ART OF SUGARCRAFT series. He has plans for more books in the future.

An active member of the British Sugarcraft Guild and the Chef and Cooks Circle, Nicholas now spends more time judging competitions than entering them. He has an ambition to run his own school of cake decorating, so that he can share his skills as a sugarcraft artist.

INTRODUCTION

Filigree

In filigree work, an outline is piped or run out to act as a border and support. The area inside is then piped with various designs and patterns, from the easiest cornelli work to complicated designs. Filigree can be used for the total decoration on a cake; side pieces, wings and centrepiece.

Careful design is important if creating new pieces. How fragile will the piece be? Will it support its own weight? Is it in scale with the cake? These are some of the questions which will need to be considered.

Lace

In this technique, royal icing is piped to resemble real lace. Copy designs from purchased or old lace, pattern books or make your own. The pieces are attached flat or standing out from the cake surface. It may take some practice to get used to handling such small delicate items.

ROYAL ICING

Albumen powder method

Albumen powder is available in pure or substitute forms. Pure 100% dried albumen is used for fine lace work. Icing made with substitute albumen is only suitable for basic work.

15ml (3 teaspoons) 100% pure albumen powder
75ml (3fl oz/⅓ cup) cold water
450g (1lb/4 cups) sifted icing (confectioner's) sugar

Dissolve albumen powder in the cold water and leave to stand for about 30 minutes, stirring every few minutes. Put the sugar in the bowl of an electric mixer, add the dissolved albumen powder, and mix using the beater for 12-15 minutes.

Fresh egg white method

1 large egg white which has been cracked and left to liquify at room temperature for about 2 hours
300g (10oz/2½ cups) finely sifted icing (confectioner's) sugar
pinch tartaric acid (cream of tartar)

If you have a heavy duty mixer use it. If not, mix icing by hand, as a lightweight hand-held mixer will not work.

Place egg white in a large bowl. Gradually stir in half the sugar until the mixture is the consistency of unwhipped cream. Add the rest of the sugar a spoonful at a time, stirring after each addition. Mix on slowest speed or stir by hand for about 5 minutes. Add tartaric acid (cream of tartar) and mix or stir until icing stands in firm peaks when spoon is withdrawn.

Hints and tips

Always leave royal icing in a covered bowl for at least two hours before using.

For piping lace or filigree, work the icing in a small bowl or on the work surface to remove any small air bubbles.

Use a fine sieve, kept for this purpose only, for sifting sugar.

Calcium is put in some brands of icing (confectioner's) sugar to keep it fine and stop it from forming lumps. However, it can also stop the icing from drying properly. To test various brands for the amount of calcium they contain, put 5ml (1tsp) of each into a separate glass of cold water. Use the sugar that leaves the water clearest.

Use very small piping bags as the small tubes used for fine work will break the bag if it is too large or too full.

EQUIPMENT

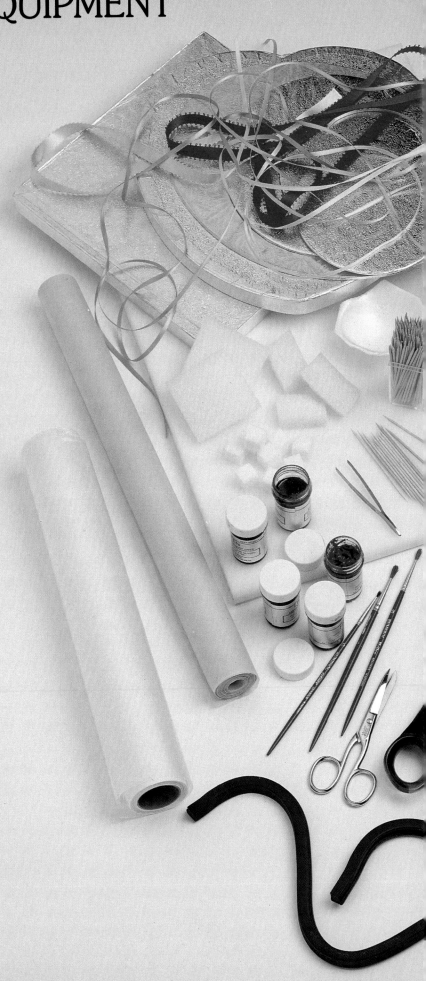

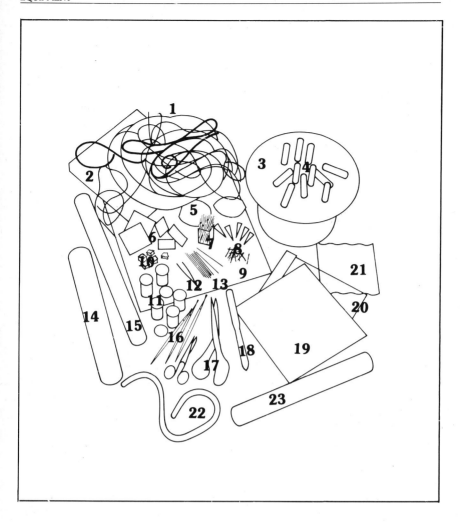

This is a selection of tools and equipment used for lace and filigree work. Most are ordinary kitchen or household items, while the more unusual tools are available from cake decorating shops and specialist shops.

1 Ribbons
2 Cake boards and cards
3 Turntable
4 Petal dust
5 Apple trays for drying curved pieces
6 Small pieces of foam or sponge
7 Cocktail sticks
8 Piping tubes
9 Pins
10 Sugar cubes to support pieces while drying
11 Paste colours
12 Tweezers
13 Nonstick work surface
14 Waxed paper
15 Greaseproof paper
16 Paintbrushes
17 Scissors
18 Palette knife
19 Strong cellophane
20 Cake tilter, which can also be used for tracing patterns
21 Leaf former for drying curved pieces
22 Flexible curve
23 Roasting wrap

PIPING TUBES

No2, 1, 0, and 00 piping tubes are used for filigree and lace work. It is worth investing in the more expensive seamless tubes for this delicate piping.

Wash new tubes in a mild detergent to remove any oil which may have been left on. If not removed, it will discolour icing and may cause it to separate.

Always clean tubes as soon as you are finished with them. Use small tube brushes or keep a paintbrush for this purpose only. Place the tubes in warm water with a little detergent and remove the icing with the brush. Make sure you can see through the tiny hole in the end. Never stick a pin or sharp object into the tube to clean it.

WAXED PAPER AND CELLOPHANE

Lace and filigree pieces are piped onto waxed paper or cellophane. Choice of paper is important as it can be hard to remove pieces.

There are many brands and qualities of waxed paper available from supermarkets and cake decorating shops. It is not always price that determines the quality. Fine waxed paper is best for lace and filigree.

Make sure that the paper has a shiny, waxed surface on both sides (double-faced). If the paper has a shiny side and a dull side this means it is single faced and only the shiny side should be used.

Cellophane is good for this sort of work; experiment with various thicknesses. Keep cellophane wrapping from gift boxes, etc for making smaller pieces.

PIPING BAGS

Well-made piping bags from greaseproof paper or baking parchment are essential for good piping. Paper bags are easier to control than the plastic or metal icing syringes, and they are disposable, so do not have to be cleaned like the plastic or nylon bags.

Piping bags should never be made too large, as they will be difficult to control and the heat from your hand will change the consistency of the icing. Bags for buttercream will need to be larger than those for royal icing. If doing a lot of piping, make several bags before starting to pipe. If piping with different coloured icing or when using different tubes, you will need several bags on hand for each one.

There are different methods for making paper piping bags. The one shown here produces bags which are a good shape and easy to use.

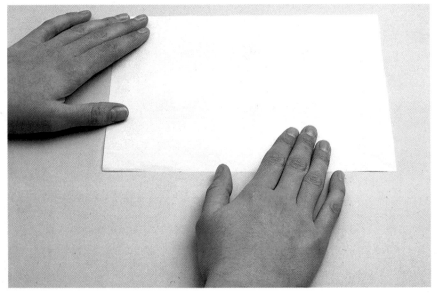

Cut a piece of greaseproof paper twice as long as it is wide.

Fold the paper diagonally. The points will not meet.

Cut along the fold with a sharp
knife to make two right-angle
triangles.

Lay the triangle flat with the right
angle facing you and fold the
corner inwards.

Place the corner on the point of
the right angle, making a cone.

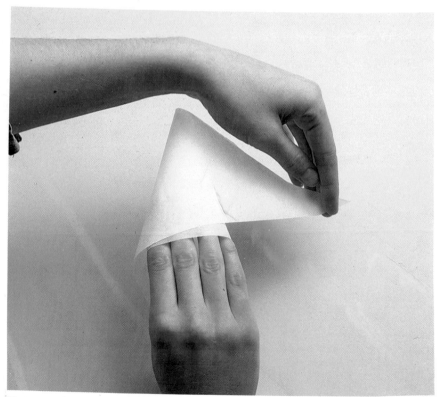

Put your fingers in the cone to
hold it and bring the other corner
over it.

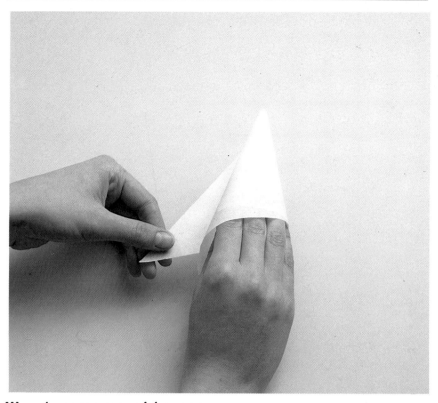

Wrap the corner around the cone
twice so that the points meet.

Slide the three points together to
tighten the bag.

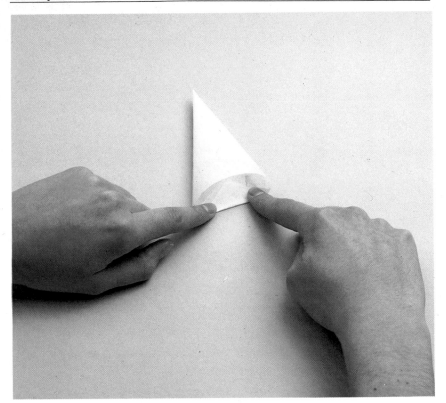

Fold the top point into the bag. If piping without a tube, fill the bag now.

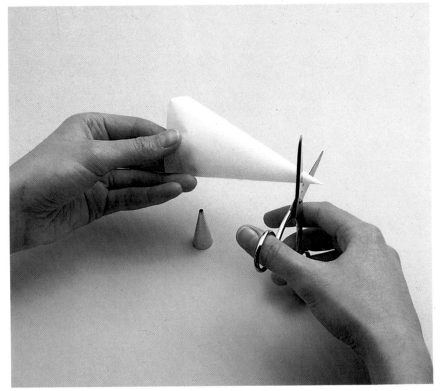

If using a piping tube, cut off the tip of the bag with scissors and insert the tube.

FILLING THE BAG

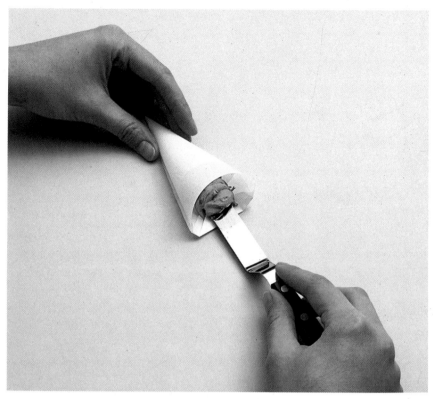

Hold the bag in your hand or place on the table and hold the point. Scoop up some icing with a palette knife and place in the bag.

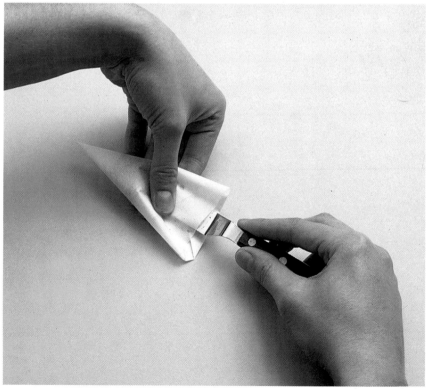

Hold the top of the bag down and gently pull out the palette knife.

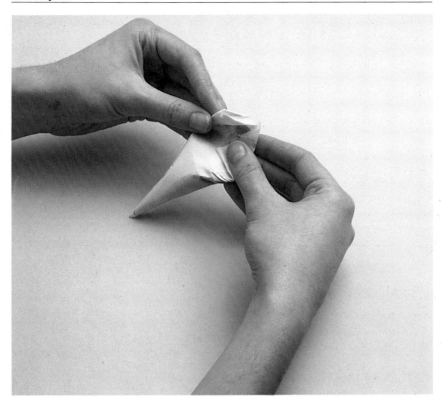

Fold the points of the bag towards the centre.

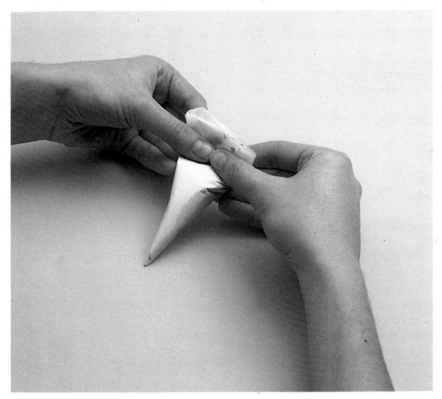

Fasten by folding the top of the bag over twice.

TECHNIQUES

Colouring icing

Most filigree and lace work is white but it is possible to make it in a colour to match the cake, table decorations, dresses, etc.

When colouring icing for this type of work, always use dust colours. Most paste and syrup colours contain glycerine, and liquid colours will stop the icing drying.

Make sure you colour enough icing to complete the work, as matching colours later can be difficult.

Mix the powder into the icing, cover with a damp cloth or lid and leave the colour to develop for about ten minutes. Several colours, especially yellow, will dry darker than they appear in the bowl. Be careful when using blue and mauve, as these tend to fade quickly when dry.

Let piped pieces dry, then store away from bright sunlight so the colour does not fade.

Several colours can be used to pipe one piece of work. This takes time as three to five bags of different coloured icing are used on a tiny piece of lace.

An alternative to colouring icing is to make white or pale cream pieces and shade them with petal dust or lustre colour when dry. Dust the colour on the dried work with a No3 or 4 soft paintbrush. This is best done on waxed paper, which will stop the piece from moving about. Once dusted, remove from paper.

Because royal icing absorbs moisture from the atmosphere, piped lace and filigree pieces are sensitive to the weather. On moist days the work can become crumbly and break easily. Therefore fine work such as attaching tiny pieces of sugar lace to a cake should be done on as dry a day as possible.

Lace and filigree can be made well in advance. Once dry, store between sheets of tissue paper. Do not use cotton wool as the points can catch and break. Store pieces in a cake box or other cardboard box, not sealed into an airtight tin or plastic container. Store the container in an airing cupboard or near a heat source. Try to keep them at a constant temperature. Storage in a room heated by day and cold at night can cause breakages to fine work.

Most lace pieces are about the size of a fingernail. When designing these small lace pieces, check the scale. Make sure they will not look too large or too small. If being attached around the side of a cake, calculate the size carefully so that a gap or an overlap does not occur.

There are two main types of lace pieces. The type with a straight top line is easier to handle and to attach to the cake. The second type, freestyle (for example the bow), is not as strong. It is attached with two small dots of icing instead of a line.

PEACOCK CAKE

This magnificent cake is decorated
with a peacock whose tail is made
from over 70 pieces of multi-
coloured lace.

MAKING LACE PIECES

Successful lace piping takes a lot of practice, especially when making many pieces of identical lace. Choose a design with several joins to begin with, and make a multiple template, as shown here. It is worth using good quality paper or card, as the template can then be used many times. Have paper and several filled piping bags ready.

Lace can be piped in advance and stored in a cake box kept in a cool, dry place until you are ready to attach it to the cake. Because it is light, several layers of lace on waxed paper can be stored on top of each other. Never seal lace in a plastic box or airtight tin. Handle lace with your fingers, never with tweezers, which will break the delicate work. Always make fresh icing to attach lace to the cake.

Draw half a piece of lace on a piece of paper using a pencil. Copy the half piece onto tracing paper. Turn over and transfer design back to the first piece of paper, ending up with a whole lace piece. The reason for the tracing is to ensure that the two sides are identical.

Make a tracing of the whole piece and transfer to thick paper or thin card. Repeat design to make 8-50 lace pieces. Once traced, go over with a pen to make a permanent template.

Stick a piece of waxed paper over the template. Use a small piping bag fitted with a No0 or 00 piping tube. Start with the straight line and work towards the pointed end.

Repeat until all the pieces on the template have been piped. Transfer carefully to a flat surface to dry.

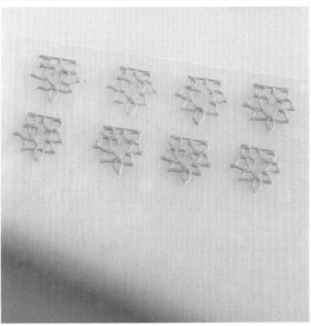

Dry lace pieces ready for attaching to the cake.

LACE DESIGNS

The photographs and templates on the following pages show a variety of different designs for lace. When choosing a lace design, consider how it will fit in with the overall design of the cake. Although certain designs, such as hearts and bells, are traditional for a wedding cake, try snowflake lace for a winter wedding, or use lace which reflects the couple's interests, such as musical or sporting designs.

Remember that lace which looks simple may not always be the easiest to do. Lace which has several short lines and joins will be stronger than that which has fewer lines. Always pipe more lace than the design of the cake calls for. If the cake is to be delivered, always take some extra lace on waxed paper and a filled piping bag wrapped in plastic as lace often gets damaged or drops off.

Always use freshly made royal icing to attach and pipe lace. Old icing will not produce strong lace, and will not hold it firmly on the cake.

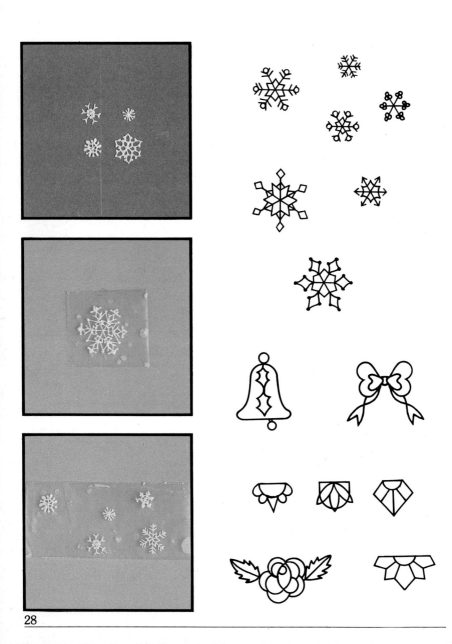

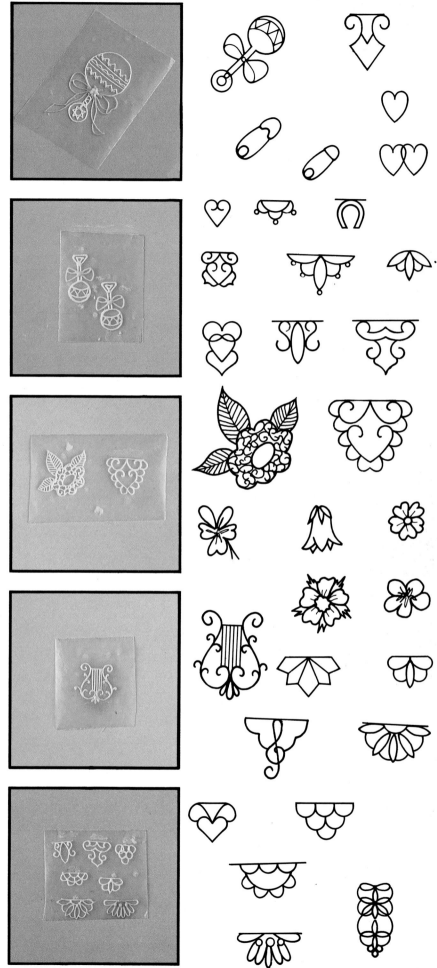

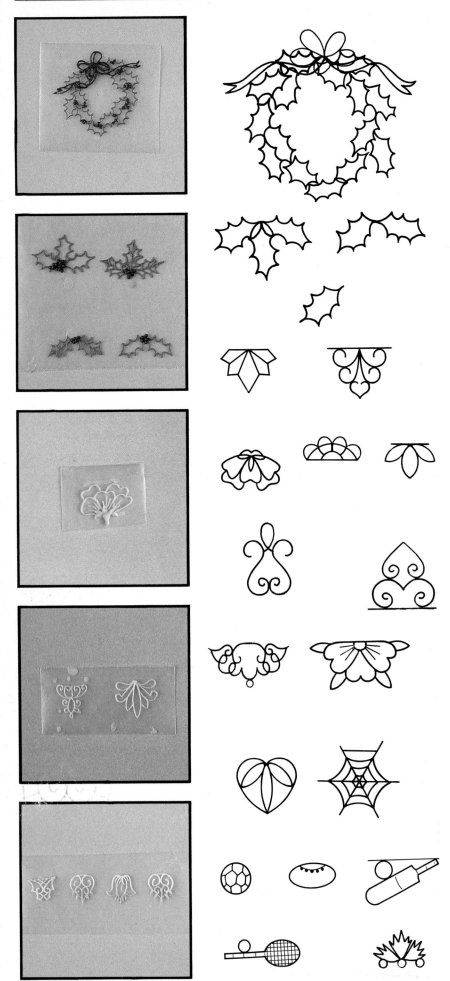

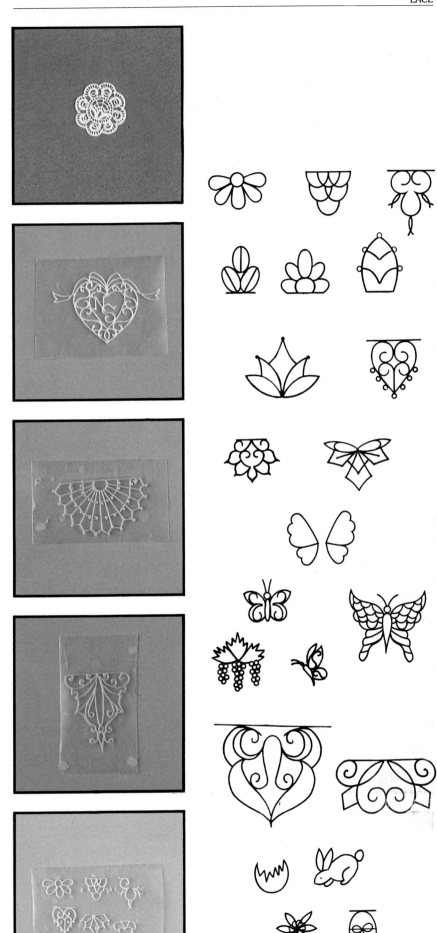

TWO-TONE LACE

These two- and three-tone lace pieces are stunning but they will take longer to pipe than single-colour lace as you must keep changing icing bags. Have all the bags filled and ready before you begin. Colour the icing with petal dust.

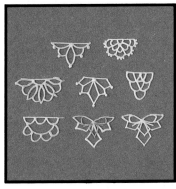

PEACOCK WITH LACE TAIL

Make tracing of peacock from the template. Scribe onto cake with scriber or hat pin, repeating pattern as shown. Mix five small containers of colour: lime green, apple green, jade, blue-mauve and turquoise. Pipe 75 tail pieces from the pattern. Pipe from centre ring to outer scallop using No0 tube in this order: lime, apple, jade, blue-mauve. Pipe a blue-mauve bulb at the top, followed by a turquoise crescent.

When dry, dust with gold lustre colour. Pipe a pair of white dragonfly wings with a No00 tube. Dry, then dust with gold lustre. Pipe body, attach wings and dry supported with foam.

Pipe peacock body by piping lines with various colours in small areas. Use a small paintbrush to texture icing and give a feathery look. Pipe white eye with black pupil and black beak. Pipe lines to establish shape of the tail. Pipe more lines inside and use a brush to feather. Place a lace piece at the end of each one, starting at the bottom and working up. The last smaller pieces are piped directly on the cake. Pipe feet with brown icing.

Dragon-fly wings used on Peacock cake

Peacock body

Tail-pieces -

pipe approximately
75 pieces

PIPING CURVED LACE

Lace can be dried on a former or over a length of pipe or dowel to make it curve. Larger designs, such as the one shown step-by-step here, work best for this although it is possible to use smaller designs. Use curved lace pieces to make flowers, or place around a cake like flat lace.

Have everything ready before you begin to work so that the finished lace can be placed on the former as soon as it is piped. If the piece starts to set, it will crack if you try to curve it.

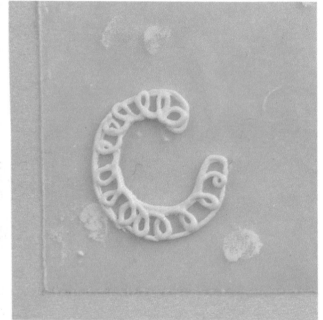

Choose a suitable design, cover with waxed paper and begin to pipe using a No0 tube. This design incorporates lace and filigree, and is best piped in sections as shown.

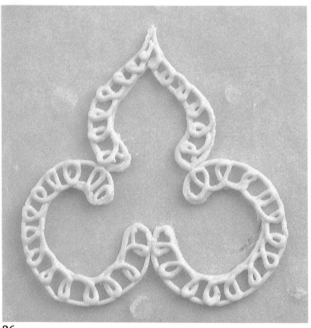

Finish the outlines of the design. Work quickly so that the icing does not start to harden.

Pipe the filigree work inside, using a different colour icing if wished.

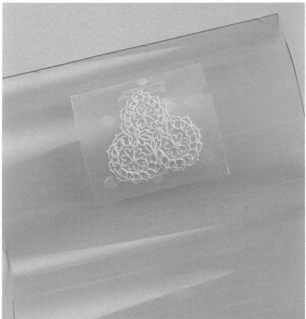

Place the finished piece over a plastic former and leave until completely dry. Lift off the waxed paper carefully and position on the cake.

Two more attractive curved lace designs. Different curves can be made by drying the pieces either in the curve of the former or over the curve.

MEDIUM-SIZED FLAT PIECES

Medium-sized flat lace pieces can be used in many different ways, depending on the design. Like smaller lace pieces, they can be placed round the sides of a cake, either flat or standing out. Flat lace also looks attractive as a border around the bottom edges of the cake. Choose a design with a straight top edge, then attach to the cake upsidedown. Flat lace can be used to make pretty designs on top of the cake or on a plaque.

Although fewer large pieces will be needed, they are extremely fragile and it will still be necessary to pipe extra pieces, as with small lace.

Choose lace designs with short lines and several joins, rather than a pattern with flowing lines. It is possible to enlarge tiny lace patterns by redrawing them on graph paper. Always dry lace completely before removing from the waxed paper. If you are nervous of removing larger pieces with your fingers, carefully slide a palette knife under the piece. Never use tweezers, which will crack the delicate work.

The design shown here is excellent because it can be piped in sections. Pipe from the centre outwards, and pipe in the direction of the curves. These are the first two stages.

The third stage of piping and the finished flat lace piece. This design would look attractive combined with small lace based on the bottom section of the piece.

CROSS-STITCH CAKE

Delicate, flowered filigree wings top this pale peach-coloured round cake. The top design is a filigree cross-stitch plaque.

CROSS-STITCH PLAQUE

This design was taken from a
cross-stitch embroidery pattern.
Once all the trellis work is finished,
pipe small dots to match the
pattern, using the colours shown.

OVAL FLOWER BASKET

This filigree plaque in different colours takes several hours to pipe. It would look best placed on the top of a white or pastel cake.

The freehand cracked ice background was piped with a No00 tube. Pipe flowers using a No0 tube.

This runout and filigree flower centrepiece could be picked up in colour with green stems and leaves and multi-coloured flowers.

PINK BRIDAL PLAQUE

This plaque shows a modern
bridal runout and filigree in an
interesting combination. Adding
touches of colour lifts the whole
effect.

WHITE LACE HEART

This runout heart was piped and left to dry. Peel off waxed paper and place on a clean piece of waxed paper, over the template. Pipe lace edging design using No0 and 00 tubes. A runout or a spray of sugar flowers could be added to the heart, or pipe an inscription.

Oval basket plaque template

Pink bridal plaque template

Rose cross-stitch design taken
from embroidery book

White lace heart template

TRELLIS SIDE DESIGNS

Cut a circle of greaseproof paper the same size as the cake; fold in quarters. Place on cake and mark where the folds meet the edge. Pipe a line from the top down the side to stick wings onto.

Pipe four dropped lines onto the top and side of the cake as shown using a No1 piping tube. Repeat on remaining three sections.

Pipe the vertical lines of the trellis on scallops in all sections.

To pipe horizontal lines, tilt the cake towards you. A tilting turntable is ideal; alternatively put something like a roll of tape under the edge of the cake board to slightly raise the edge you are working on. Hold tube close to cake so lines do not droop.

Pipe angled lines starting with the left-to-right lines. Keep the angle the same throughout.

Pipe opposite angled lines on all sections.

Pipe a small shell around top and base of each scallop with No2 tube. Pipe a line following each scallop, and two dots at each point.

Finish the cake by piping a shell border around the base. Outline with dot edging. A ribbon can be placed around the board if wished.

HEART CAKE

A trellis-work heart tops this small engagement or Valentine's Day cake. The side designs also incorporate trellis work.

TRELLIS WORK

A heart is a simple popular shape
for any occasion.

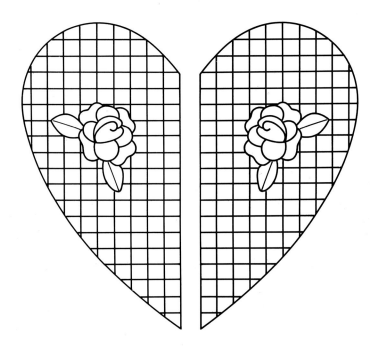

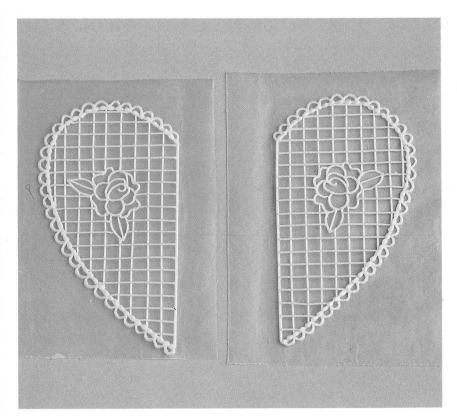

Make two halves. Pipe outline
with No1 tube, pipe rose design
followed by trellis with a No1,
then the scalloped edge with a
No0.

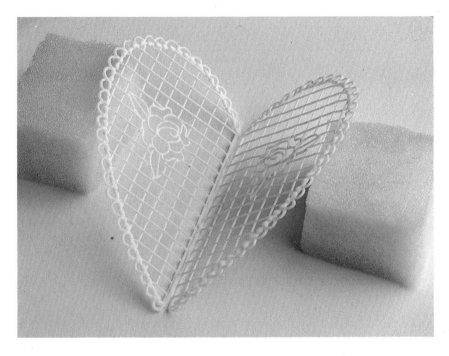

Pipe a line down centre of cake with No2 tube. Place two halves in position touching. Support with foam and dry for two hours. Remove foam.

Place 3mm (⅛in) ribbon down centre to neaten the join. Attach a few pink flowers to cake. Pipe some green leaves and a small dove.

FILIGREE FLOWERS

Filigree work can be used to create all kinds of lovely flowers, such as the pansy and daffodil shown here. Use white icing and dust with colour when dry, or colour the icing with petal dust before piping. The flowers can be placed individually on a cake, or they can be wired into sprays. Filigree flowers are extremely fragile, so take care when wiring.

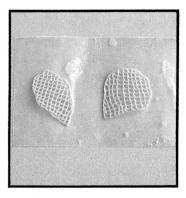

Pansy

Pipe the five petals on waxed paper as shown. Set the top two petals *over* a curve. Set the other three *into* a curve. Once dry, assemble on waxed paper with a little royal icing. Let dry, then dust mauve and yellow.

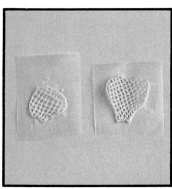

Daffodil

Pipe three of each of the two template petals onto waxed paper. Place the broader petals *over* a curve and the three other petals *in* a curve. Grease a piping tube and pipe the trumpet onto it. Remove all six petals from the paper when dry. Hold piping tube in front of heat source to remove trumpet.

Pipe a small circle of yellow royal icing on waxed paper. Place the three broader curved petals evenly in position. Place the other three petals in position curving upwards. Put trumpet in the centre with royal icing. Add five stamens; let dry.

Dust trumpet with orange petal dust. To use in a spray, or as shown, stick a wire and floristry tape leaf behind flower.

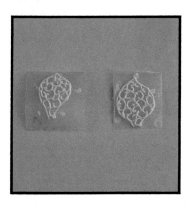

Daffodil - pipe 3 of each petal

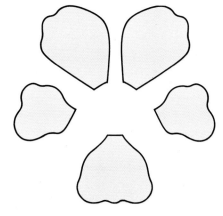

Pansy - pipe 1 of each petal

BRIAR ROSE

This briar rose has been used to
decorate the filigree box.

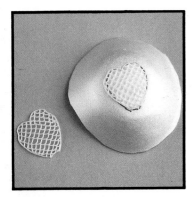

Trace the template onto the base of
five shallow polystyrene apple trays.
Grease with white fat (shortening) and
pipe the petal outline, then pipe a
freehand fishscale pattern using a No0
tube.

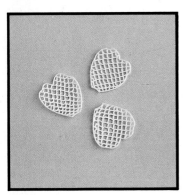

After drying for two hours,
remove petals by placing tray in front
of a heat source to melt the fat.

Dust the lower third of each petal with
pink petal dust. Pipe a small circle of
white royal icing on waxed paper and
assemble the petals onto it. Use
tweezers to add some yellow floristry
stamens to the centre. Let dry.

Pipe some leaves on waxed paper
using a No0 tube and green icing.
Place immediately over a curved
surface to dry in a natural shape.
Leave to dry, then remove from paper.

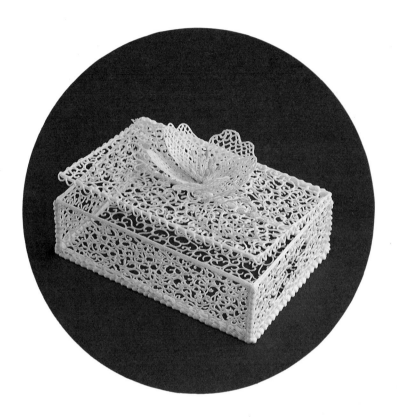

Briar rose and leaf templates
to go with filigree box

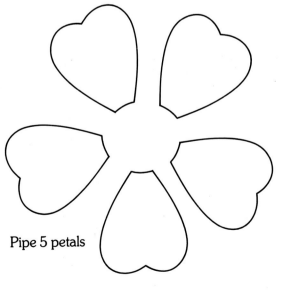

Pipe 5 petals

Pipe 3-5 leaves

FILIGREE BOX

This filigree box with briar rose and leaves makes a lovely decoration for the top of a cake. If you plan to fill it with chocolates, make the base a solid runout as filigree would collapse under the weight of the sweets.

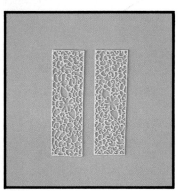

The base and lid are exactly the same size. Pipe the lid and base, the two long sides and the two end pieces on waxed paper using a No0 tube. Let dry, then remove from paper and turn over onto foam. Pipe the outer line on the reverse side to give support. Leave to dry.

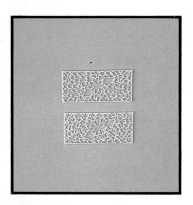

Two long side pieces

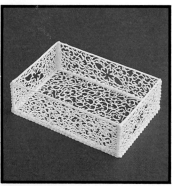

Two end pieces

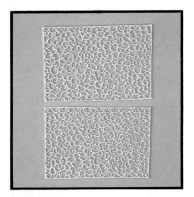

Assemble directly on the cake or plaque. Stick down the base with dots of icing at the corners. Pipe a line of icing along the base and place the four sides in position. Pipe a small snailstrail along the base and up the four side seams. Let dry for two hours.

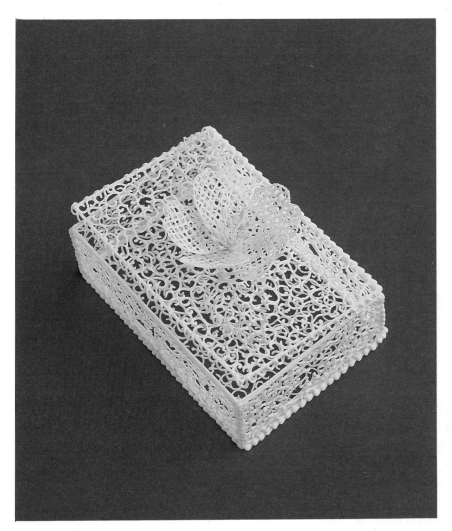

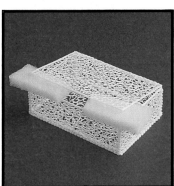

Pipe a double line along one of the top edges to act as a hinge. Place lid in position, support open with two pieces of foam. Let dry for two hours.

Remove foam and pipe a scallop along the top edge. Stick briar rose and leaves into position with a little royal icing.

Lid and base - pipe 2

Filigree box template

Sides - pipe 2 of each

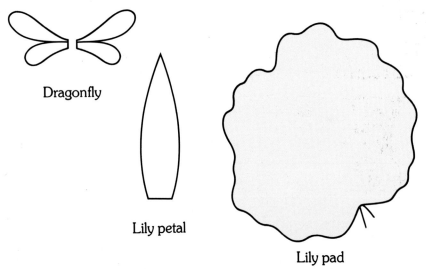

Dragonfly

Lily petal

Lily pad

WATER-LILY AND PAD

Follow the directions for the filigree briar rose. You will need 12-20 petals so use five polystyrene apply trays to save time. Draw the petal on the tray, grease with white fat (shortening) and pipe the outline using a No0 tube and a suitable colour. Pipe the fine trellis. Let dry, then remove petal by holding tray in front of a heat source which will melt the fat.

Pipe the pad in green using a freehand S&C scroll design. Dry flat.

Pipe a pair of dragonfly wings using a No00 tube.

To assemble, place pad onto cake surface and stick with a little royal icing. Pipe a ring of icing the same shade as the lily at the stalk end of the pad. Place five or six petals in position in the ring; support with small pieces of foam. Dry for a few minutes then continue placing petals into the lily. Finish by adding some floristry stamens to the centre.

Pipe blue body of the dragonfly on waxed paper. Put two wings in position, support with foam and dry. Dust body with lustre dust and place on the tip of a petal with a little icing.

LARGE CHRISTMAS TREE

Pipe one whole tree using a No1 tube for the outline and a No0 for the fishscale filigree. When dry, turn over and pipe the main lines again. Let dry.

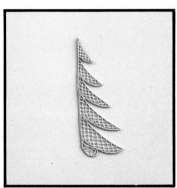

Pipe four half trees. Let dry, then turn over and re-pipe the main lines. Let dry.

To assemble, pipe a line down the centre of the whole tree using a No1 tube and the same green icing. Pipe another line directly beside it. Place two of the half sections in position as shown, supporting with foam. Let dry for an hour.

Stand tree up. Pipe two more lines down the centre. Place the final pieces in position. Let dry.

SMALL CHRISTMAS TREE

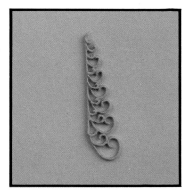

Pipe six tree halves using a No1 tube. When dry, turn over and re-pipe all the lines on the other side. Let dry.

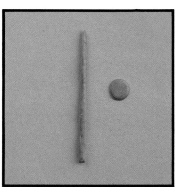

Outline stem with a No1 tube and flood using slightly softened green icing. Pipe a circle and run out for the base. When stem is dry, pipe the other side. Let dry.

Assemble the stem on the base, support while drying. Place the six pieces around the stem and let dry.

When the tree is completely dry, carefully remove from the waxed paper.

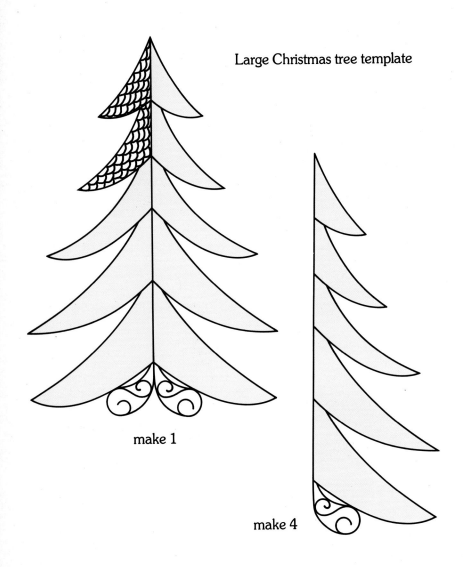

Large Christmas tree template

make 1

make 4

Small Christmas tree template

make 6

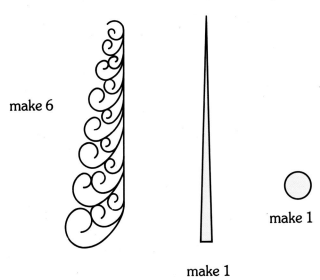

make 1

make 1

Large Christmas tree. This design could be adapted to make an unusual side decoration for a square Christmas cake. Pipe two side pieces and the main piece, then attach to the side of the cake. A larger than usual board will be needed to support the trees.

Small Christmas tree. To make a whole forest of Christmas trees, vary the sizes of the templates. Pipe some trees in white and dust with silver snowflake to give a wintery look. The trees could be placed on a Christmas cake, or on small cards or sugarpaste plaques and used as place markers.

FILIGREE GIRL CAKE

A little girl made in pink filigree tops this heart-shaped birthday cake. Even the flowers are freestanding filigree pieces.

FILIGREE LADY

The pink lady is assembled on a heart cake, but she could be assembled on a plaque which could be removed and kept as a souvenir.

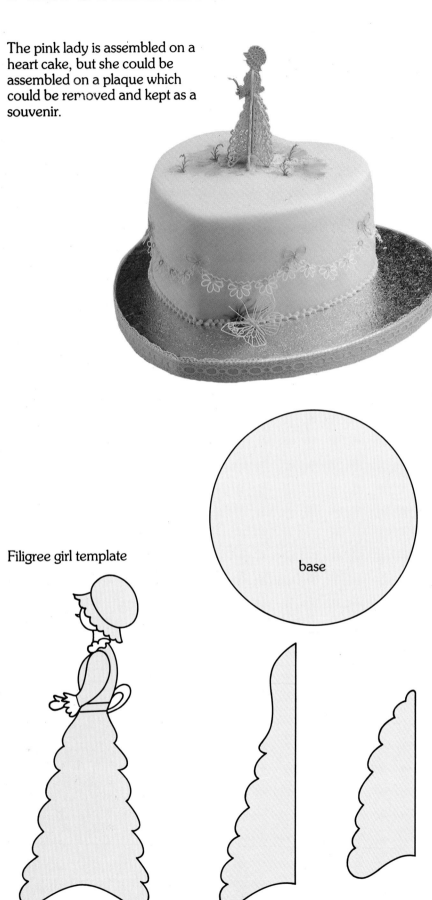

Filigree girl template

base

Main body

Body - pipe 2

Skirt - pipe 4

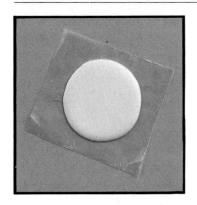

Run out a round plaque.

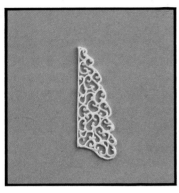

Pipe four skirt pieces. When dry, turn over and pipe the main outline on the other side.

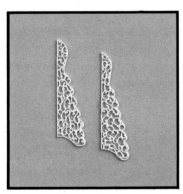

Pipe two long body pieces. When dry, turn over and re-pipe.

Pipe one main body piece and again turn over and re-pipe when dry. Pipe hands and face outlines in white or flesh colour and let dry.

To assemble, stick main body on plaque or cake. Put the two long sides into position. Attach the four small skirt pieces. If using a plaque, pipe petit point lace around the edge.

RATTLE

This rattle could decorate a
christening cake or a first-birthday
cake.

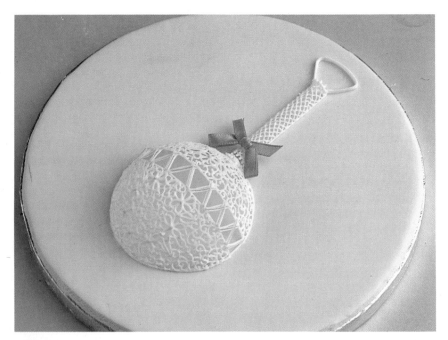

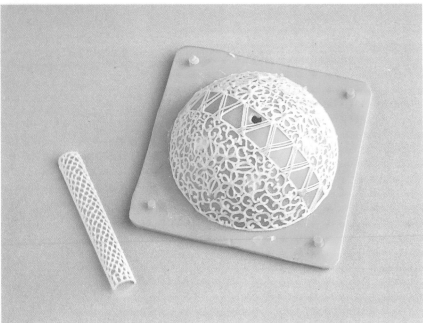

Grease a wooden dowel and pipe
the stem of the rattle. Leave to
dry. Pipe a filigree design over
the surface of a large greased
flower former or apple tray. Let
dry. Hold dowel in front of heat
source to release stem; do the
same for the main part of the
rattle. Stick the dome with a few
small dots of icing. Place stem in
position and pipe handle with a
No2 tube. Finish off with a bow.

CRADLE

This cradle, suitable for a christening cake, can be left empty or filled with a sugar baby, quilt, etc.

All the pieces are piped with a No1 tube.

Pipe miniature dove wings and tail onto waxed paper using pink icing and No0 tube.

Use the templates to make the pieces of the cradle. For each piece, pipe the solid outline first, then fill with runout icing. When the runout outline is dry, pipe the trellis design. This shows the finished head piece.

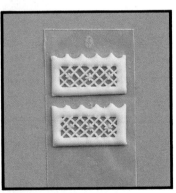

The sides of the basket of the cradle piped onto individual rectangles of waxed paper.

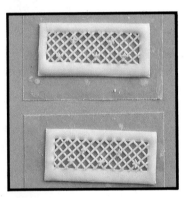

The sides of the canopy of the cradle. When all the pieces of the cradle are dry, pipe on miniature flowers using pink icing and No0 tube.

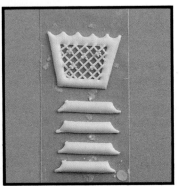

The foot of the cradle and the four rocker pieces. When the runout rockers are dry, stick together to make two finished rockers.

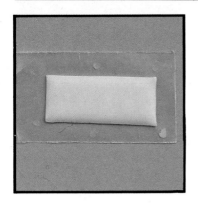

Make a solid runout base and let dry. Assemble the cradle on waxed paper. Attach head and foot pieces first and support with piping tubes. When dry, position side pieces and support. Carefully position canopy.

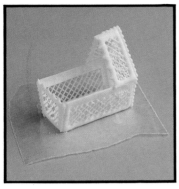

When pieces are assembled, pipe a small shell along all the edges. Decorate with the miniature doves. Pipe the dove body onto the cradle, then add wings and tail. Place the rockers on a sugarpaste plaque and attach the cradle on top of them. If wished, fill the cradle with a sugarpaste pillow and blanket and a tiny modelled baby.

Cradle template

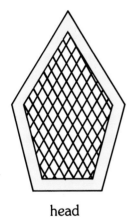

head

solid runout base

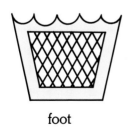

foot

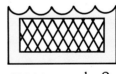

canopy - make 2

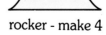

rocker - make 4

top

sides - make 2

CROWN CAKE

A pretty mauve cake is topped
with a filigree crown. Leave the
crown plain, or fill with sugar or
silk flowers.

FILIGREE CROWN

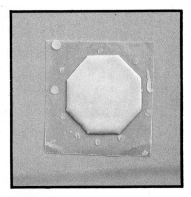

Outline base with a No1 tube and flood.

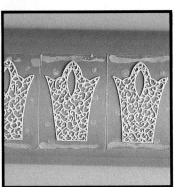

To make the eight filigree pieces, pipe outline with No1 tube. Place over plastic pipe, then pipe a freehand S&C scroll filigree design into the space. Dry all pieces.

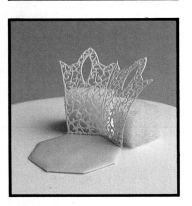

Stick the octagonal base onto the cake or plaque. Pipe a line along one side of the octagon and place on a filigree piece. Use a piece of foam to support. Repeat with the next piece. Pull both pieces down so the two points touch and support at this angle. Pipe a small shell on the inside edge to strengthen and give a neat edge.

Continue with the other six pieces to complete the crown. Support each piece with foam. Leave for two hours.

The crown can be filled with a spray of pale pink carnations, mauve freesias and blossom.

When the crown is in position, complete the top designs on the cake. Place a ribbon around the middle.

Pipe pale mauve lace with the same icing used to coat the cake. Attach as shown and leave to dry.

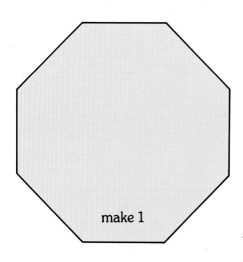

Filigree crown - make 8

make 1

Runout octagonal base for filigree crown

WINGS

Fragile sugar-lace wings give a dramatic finish to a cake. They are a bit tricky to handle and transport because they protrude from the cake. When designing lace wings, a balanced shape and main structural support are necessary, otherwise the wing could collapse when placed on the cake.

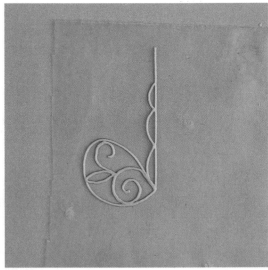

Stick a piece of waxed paper on the chosen design. Pipe the top piece of the design using a No0 tube.

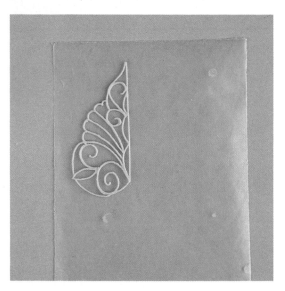

Continue piping until the top side is finished.

Pipe the other side piece.

The finished wing with its three main pieces. Once dry, carefully remove from the waxed paper using a crank handled palette knife. Turn over onto a piece of foam which will act as a support and stop the wing moving about. Pipe the design on the other side to strengthen. Let wing dry before using, or store flat on thin foam.

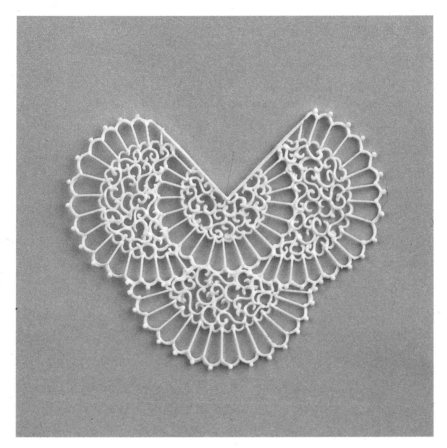

A double piped filigree wing as
featured on the peach cake with
cross-stitch plaque.

Flower and foliage lace wing, all
piped with a No0 tube.

WINGED CROWN CAKE

Elegant pointed wings top a small
hexagonal cake. For a different
look, the wings could be placed
flat on the cake.

WINGED CROWN

This design works best on a hexagonal cake as each of the six wings points to a corner making it easy to position them. You will need six of each of the two lace designs. The bunch of flowers is dried flat and the top pieces dried over a curve.

Three left and three right wings are needed. Pipe the outline onto waxed paper with a No1 tube, and the inside filigree with a No0. Transfer to a flat surface to dry. Another method is to make three copies of each wing pattern. The piped design can then stay on top of the pattern until it dries. When dry, turn over on foam and re-pipe the outer line only. Let dry. Pipe a line about 5cm (2in) long and place a wing in position. Support both sides with foam. Place the opposite wing into position. Pipe a dot of icing on the spots marked with a cross on the template and bring to touch. Keep wings supported with foam and clean excess icing from cake before it dries. Dry for one hour. Stick remaining four wings in place. Dry for 30 minutes.

LACE INSERTS

Runout work can be given a softer look with lacy inserts. Design is important here to ensure the delicate work is not supporting the runout. Pipe the outlines, then the filigree or lace work, then flood in the runout area.

Designs for the lace inserts can be copied from fabric lace for a realistic look. Small lace pieces can be used to make pretty additions to large runout letters. Runout and lace work can be used as borders, collars, wings or flat top decorations for cakes. Handle the finished pieces carefully.

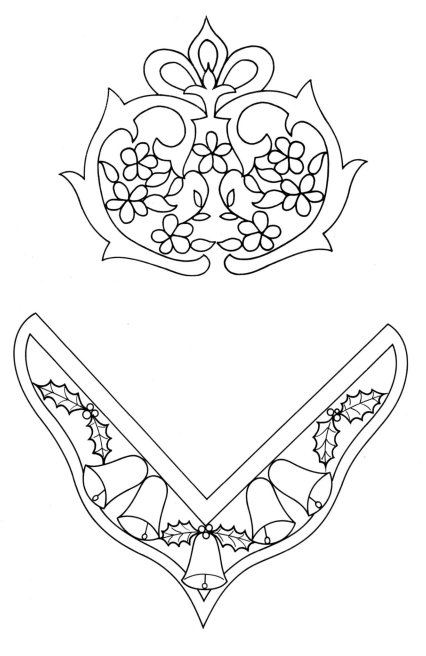

Lace makes a dainty runout
sectional collar.

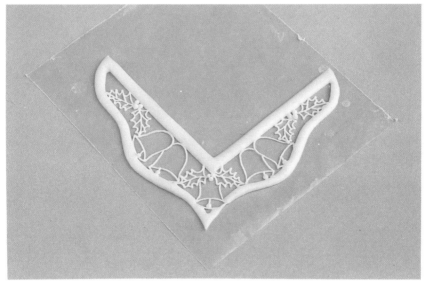

This corner section for a Christmas
cake has a runout edge with lace
work inside. It could also be done
in colour.

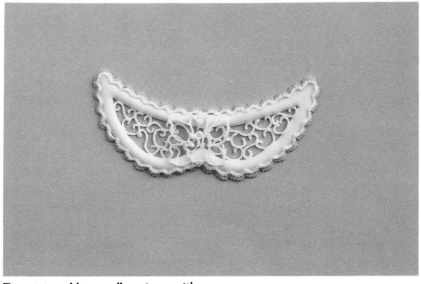

Runout and lace collar piece with
a piped lace orchid added when
dry.

COLLARS

Lace and filigree work can be used to make delicate collars. The fine piping is particularly attractive when combined with runout work, which gives the finished pieces more strength. These collars are very fragile, and choice of design is important so that the delicate work is not supporting the weight of the much heavier runout. It is a good idea to make at least one extra collar piece in case of breakages, especially if the cake must be transported.

To pipe a runout and filigree collar, pipe the runout outlines first, then do the fine lace or filigree work. Dry, then flood the runout areas. Dry the collar thoroughly before attaching to the cake.

For a filigree collar, place cellophane or waxed paper over the chosen design and pipe with a No0 or No1 tube. Dry, then turn over and pipe on the other side for greater strength. It is best to keep these collars quite small and have several pieces to go around the cake.

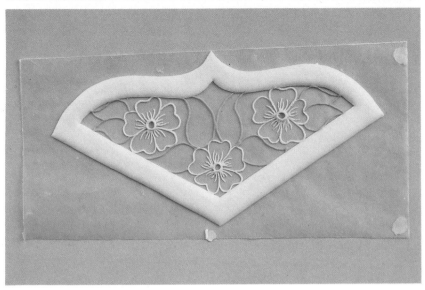

This runout collar features an inset of finely piped filigree flowers. Any flower design could be used.

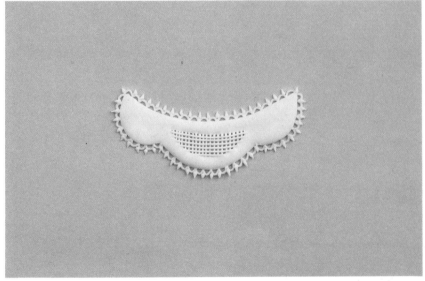

This sectional collar piece has trellis work piped with a No0 tube into the inset. More elaborate designs could also be used.

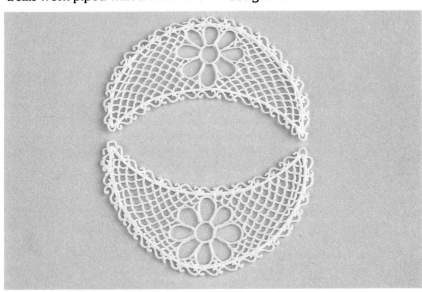

This pretty filigree collar makes a round cake into a petal. If used top and bottom, the gap between could contain piping.

HORSE AND CARRIAGE WEDDING CAKE

A miniature carriage drawn by tiny horses could top a small wedding cake, as shown, or be placed on the bottom tier of a larger wedding cake.

HORSE AND CARRIAGE

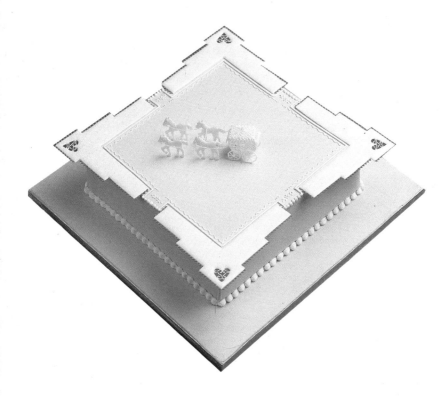

Two large and two small wheels are required.

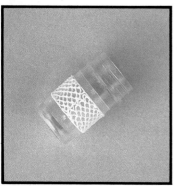

The main chassis is placed over an empty paste colour pot. Pipe quickly and neatly to ensure it is in position before icing starts to dry. Dry upright. Make sure waxed paper is only slightly larger than template or there will be an overlap.

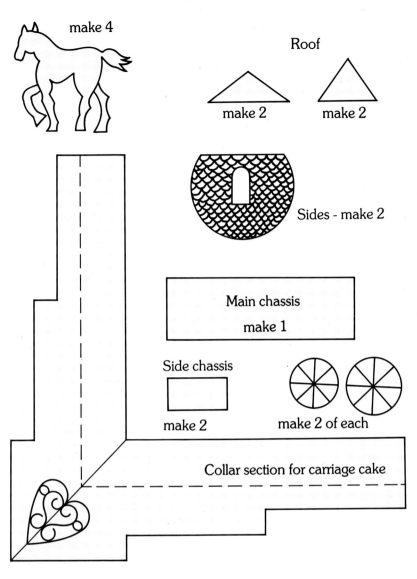

make 4

Roof

make 2   make 2

Sides - make 2

Main chassis
make 1

Side chassis

make 2

make 2 of each

Collar section for carriage cake

Pipe two small and two large roof sections.

Make four double flooded horses; pipe outline with No0 tube, flood with runout icing. When dry, turn over and runout the other side without re-piping. Let dry.

Pipe two small continuation chassis pieces, set to dry over pot as above.

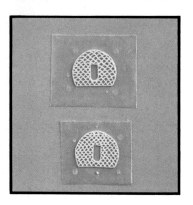

Pipe two side pieces.

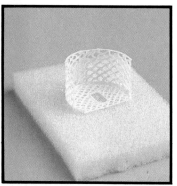

Assemble on foam to avoid breakages. Place a side piece on a flat surface and pipe a line along edge. Add main chassis piece.

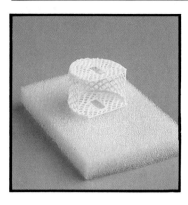

Repeat with second side piece. Dry for 15 minutes.

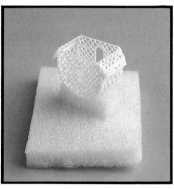

Use small scissors to cut a piece of foam to fit the curve of the chassis. Sit carriage in foam. Stick two small curved pieces and side pieces.

Place two large roof pieces in position on a line of icing, making sure they touch. Place two smaller pieces. Pipe a small shell with a No0 tube to neaten and strengthen the join.

Pipe a dropped scallop around edge and three dots in centre of roof. Let dry 15 minutes. Stick on wheels, checking they are level and straight. Dry for two hours.

Pipe manes, bridles and horses' eyes.

OLD LACE

OLD LACE

On the previous page are some pieces of old lace that would make wonderful designs to copy for sugar work. Handle antique lace with care, as it is fragile. Place piece into a plastic folder and stick waxed paper onto the plastic. Grease with white vegetable fat (shortening).

This lace is piped with a No00 tube. This is very time consuming, but it is essential to have fine lines. The icing must not be too soft or the definition of design will be lost. Add a little cream colour to give an antique look.

Once piped pieces are dry, remove carefully by holding in front of a heat source to melt fat. Carefully remove from paper with a crank handled palette knife.

SUGAR FRILL

This sugar frill makes a background for a posy of ribbons and sugar flowers. Use on top of a cake or as a party favour.

Grease a plastic posy frill with white fat (shortening). Pipe frill with a No0 tube, joining up all the sections. Leave to dry. To release, hold in front of a heat source.

ANTIQUE LACE CAKE

Suitable for a lace anniversary,
small wedding or birthday, this
delicate cake features sugar lace
copied from pieces of handmade
antique lace.

BUTTERCREAM

Buttercream can be used to pipe lace and filigree designs onto cakes, just as for royal icing. Many of the designs shown in this book can be adapted for butter-cream work.

Because buttercream does not set hard, it is not possible to use it for freestanding objects, or for lace which stands away from the cake. However, designs can be piped onto the surface of the cake and lace can be piped around the top, sides or cake board.

Use buttercream which is stiffer than coating consistency. Piping bags for buttercream work can be larger than those used for royal icing, but because the heat of your hand changes the consistency of the icing, it is better to use several small bags. Colour the buttercream with paste colours, as liquid colours will thin the icing. Although it is possible to pipe very fine work in butter-cream, the very smallest piping tubes are difficult to use. A No0 or No1 tube is the smallest tube

which will give successful results.

When piping buttercream lace or filigree on a buttercream covered cake, lightly mark the design on the cake first, using a scriber or other sharp object. Remember that it is always possible to smooth over the buttercream if the design is not successful the first time. However, coloured icing will mark the surface of the cake and will not be easy to scrape off.

Buttercream lace is piped directly onto the cake, rather than on waxed paper, so it may be difficult to duplicate the same design several times. If you do not feel confident to pipe freehand designs, choose a lace pattern which is fairly simple and trace it onto paper several times and use the tracings to scribe the design onto the cake.

Filigree in coloured buttercream can be piped onto a sugarpasted cake, or onto a cake which has been covered with melted chocolate and allowed to set.

Never store a buttercream cake in the refrigerator, as the icing will sweat and the colours will run. Buttercream does not keep for very long, and the cake should be eaten soon after decorating.

Basic buttercream

300g (10oz/1¼ cups) butter or white vegetable fat (shortening)
450g (1lb/4 cups) icing (confectioner's) sugar
45ml (3 tablespoons) cold water
flavouring and colouring

Thoroughly blend together the fat and sugar. Add cold water and flavouring and mix for about 5 minutes. Colour as desired.

Buttercream made with evaporated milk

This is a good icing for piping. It can be stored in the refrigerator for 2-3 weeks and freezes well.

225g (8oz/1 cup) white vegetable fat (shortening)
75ml (3fl oz/⅓ cup) evaporated milk
450g (1lb/4 cups) icing (confectioner's) sugar
vanilla essence (extract) to taste

Cream fat. Add the evaporated milk and beat well. Slowly add the sugar and beat until smooth and creamy. Add flavouring and beat again.

These lace designs are suitable for buttercream work. Pipe with a No1 tube.

BUTTERCREAM LACE AND FILIGREE

The practice boards show a variety of different lace and filigree designs piped with a No1 tube and buttercream. These were all piped freehand, although most of the templates in this book can be adapted for buttercream work. Try varying simple designs by using several different colours. Multi-coloured cornelli work, for example, is easy to do and very attractive. Use buttercream made with evaporated milk for fine work.

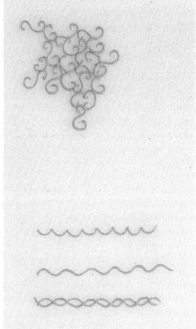

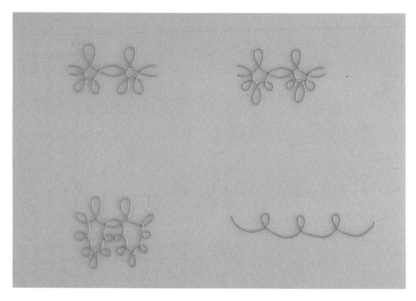

Template for Buttercream filigree cake.

BUTTERCREAM FILIGREE CAKE

This unusual cake is covered in melted chocolate and then decorated with piped buttercream filigree.

WORKING WITH CHOCOLATE

There are two types of chocolate for use in sugarcraft — baker's chocolate and couverture. Baker's chocolate, also called compound chocolate, is much easier to work with, but does not have as good a flavour as couverture, which is the purest form of chocolate. Most of the chocolate work in this book can be done using either type of chocolate. In the few ideas where couverture is required, this is clearly stated. Both types are available in plain, milk and white forms.

Baker's chocolate

Baker's chocolate is available from most supermarkets and sugarcraft suppliers in slabs or buttons. It differs from couverture in that most of the cocoa butter has been removed and replaced with a vegetable fat, eliminating the need for tempering.

To melt baker's chocolate, place in the top of a double saucepan over hand hot water and stir until melted. Heat to a temperature of 38-43°C (100-110°F), or until completely smooth, if not using a thermometer. If the chocolate gets too hot it may have fat bloom — white streaks — when unmoulded. White sugar bloom may appear if the chocolate is too cool. Never allow steam or moisture to get in contact with the chocolate, or it will thicken and become unusable.

Baker's chocolate can be placed in the refrigerator after it has set to hasten contraction. Do not put couverture in the refrigerator or it may develop bloom.

Couverture

Chocolate work done with couverture will be smooth and glossy, and the flavour will be better than baker's chocolate. However, couverture has to be tempered before use. Couverture is available from sugarcraft suppliers and some specialist food shops. Most bars of dessert chocolate are made by a different process and are not suitable for chocolate work, so be sure that the chocolate you are using is pure couverture.

There are many different methods for tempering couverture, which involves heating and then cooling the chocolate to a precise temperature so that the fat in the cocoa butter crystallizes. Well-tempered chocolate will have a high gloss and snap when set. A chocolate or clinical thermometer or sugar thermometer is necessary for tempering.

This method of tempering works for quantities up to 450g

(1lb) of plain chocolate. Break the chocolate into small pieces and melt in the top of a double saucepan over simmering, not boiling, water. When the chocolate reaches 46°C (115°F), remove the pan from the hot water and place in a bowl of cold water. Stir until the chocolate cools to 27-28°C (80-82°F), then return to the pan of hot water and heat to 31°C (88°F), when the chocolate is tempered and ready for use. If tempering milk chocolate the temperatures should be 1°C (2°F) lower at all stages.

Another method is to melt the chocolate in a double saucepan as above and heat to 46°C (115°F) for plain chocolate or 43°C (110°F) for milk. Pour two-thirds of the chocolate onto a cold marble slab and spread out with a palette knife. Work with a plastic scraper to bring the temperature down. The chocolate will begin to set at this point. Return it to the pan and reheat to 31°C (88°F) for plain or 29°C

(84°F) for milk which will take a very short time. The chocolate is ready for use.

Chocolate which is not tempered correctly will not set well, and unmoulding will be difficult. There may also be a white or grey bloom on the surface.

To thicken chocolate for piping

Melt 120g (4oz) chocolate and add 2-3 drops of glycerine to thicken. Chocolate with added glycerine will start to set quickly. If it sets in the bowl it cannot be remelted, so only thicken a small amount at a time.

To make coloured chocolate, colour white chocolate with petal dust as liquid colour thickens the chocolate too much.

Filigree heart piped with milk chocolate.

Chocolate lace designs should have fewer joins than royal icing lace, as it is more difficult to stop and start when piping melted chocolate.

FILIGREE EASTER EGG

Coloured chocolate dragonflies
and pink waterlilies are attractive
decorations for this large
chocolate Easter egg.

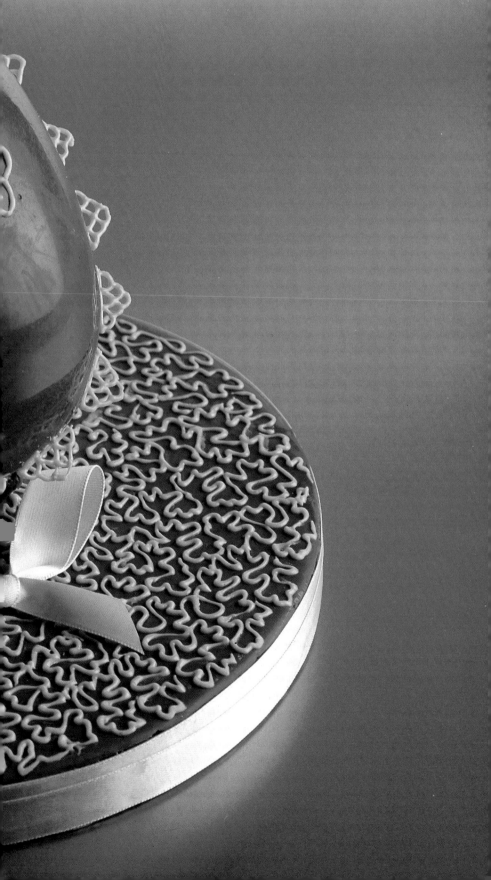

EASTER EGG

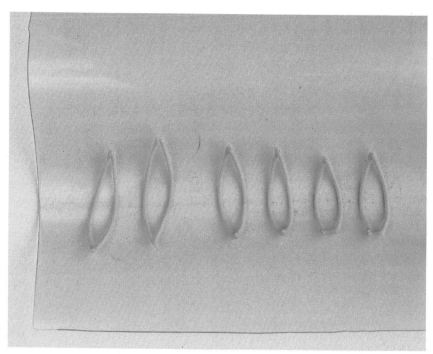

Water lily petals are piped over a curved surface.

Pipe the main piece of the water lily and the dragonfly on the outside of an Easter egg mould.

Mould a medium-sized chocolate egg. Cover a 20-25cm (8-9in) cake board with chocolate and mould a semisolid posy bowl or similar. Stick posy bowl on the board and the egg onto the posy bowl. Leave to set. Melt some white chocolate and put into three small basins. Colour and pipe from one basin at a time. With pink chocolate pipe the water lily petals and dragonfly onto the polished outer side of the mould. Pipe some separate pink petals over a curved surface. Pipe pink chocolate lace onto waxed paper. Let set at room temperature. Pipe yellow chocolate stamens and a green chocolate leaf as shown. Let set at room temperature, then place in refrigerator or freezer for a minute until chocolate contracts from the mould for easy removal. Stick onto egg along with the dragonfly. Stick additional petals onto lily at an angle. Pipe a small line of chocolate and stick on one piece of lace. Continue around edge. Pipe green chocolate cornelli work on the board before or after lace has been attached. Stick a ribbon around the board and tie a bow in front of the egg.

CHOCOLATE LACE CAKE

Pieces of piped chocolate lace
and filigree are used to decorate a
gâteau which has been covered
with buttercream icing.

BUTTERCREAM GÂTEAU WITH CHOCOLATE CENTREPIECE

The filigree pieces can be made in advance but assemble them shortly before use, as this decoration is difficult to store.

Cover gâteau with natural coloured buttercream. The first layer of icing will contain crumbs so to make sure the second coat is smooth, put cake in the refrigerator for ten minutes. Remove and leave at room temperature for five minutes before re-coating. Use a comb scraper on the top and round the side. Pipe top and bottom shells with a No44 tube; overpipe with No3, then overpipe again.

Wear cotton gloves when assembling the centrepiece as the warmth of your fingers will melt the fine pieces. Stick plaque to the gâteau as shown. Pipe a line and hold one piece in position with the central line straight. Place the opposite side in position, sticking the two together. Hold until set. Attach the other two pieces in position. Pipe bulbs of buttercream on the top for contrast.

For the disc, run out a sheet of chocolate on greaseproof paper in a baking tin. Pick up and drop paper several times so any air bubbles break. Leave until it just begins to set. Cut out a round plaque. Leave to dry.

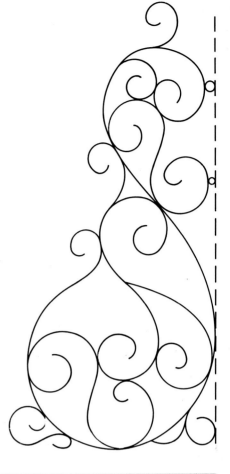

Melt some milk chocolate; thicken with a little glycerine. Pipe four pieces of the design shown onto greaseproof or waxed paper which has been well stuck down on the work surface.

BUTTERCREAM GÂTEAU WITH CHOCOLATE FILIGREE

A pretty freestanding filigree chocolate ornament stands in the centre of a buttercream covered gâteau.

Designs for chocolate
filigree centrepieces.

INSTRUCTIONS FOR CAKES

Filigree crown cake. Cover a cake with pale mauve royal icing. Make and position the crown. Pipe a small shell around the outer edge of the crown with a No1 tube. Use a No0 tube to pipe forget-me-nots freehand over the top of the cake. Pipe a shell with a No2 tube around the base of the cake. Place a contrasting ribbon around the side and attach sugar lace around the edge. The gap between pieces should be about one-quarter of the width of the piece. Fill the crown with sugar flowers and ribbons.

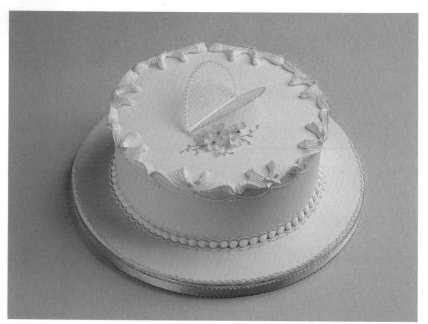

Trellis-work heart cake. Make trellis-work heart and position on a pale green royal iced cake. Divide cake top into eight. Pipe eight pairs of scrolls overpiped with trellis in darker pink. Add tiny bows. Let dry and place in position. Pipe a shell around base with No43 and dropped lines with No1. Finish with scalloped rope lines around shells and a wavy line around the edge.

122

Winged crown cake. Cover a hexagonal cake in cream sugarpaste. Place curved lace on edge of cake, sticking on a fine line of icing. Pipe a shell around base with No2. Pipe a small dot at corners and place flat lace in position. Place the crown on top of the cake.

Filigree lady cake. Cover a heart shaped cake in pale cream sugarpaste. Let dry at least two days. Make a template the height and length of one side. Fold in four and draw a scalloped line along all sections. Scribe onto both sides of heart. Pipe a herringbone around base with a No2 tube, and a small scallop on the sides. Make some daisy lace, butterfly wings, small flowers with stems and curved bow lace.

Use your fingers to smooth green royal icing on top of cake. Position filigree lady. Place flowers with stems onto the green and one in lady's hand. Stick lace around sides, then place curved lace bows in position. Finish by piping some foliage and placing butterfly in position.

123

Cross-stitch cake. Cover a round cake with apricot royal icing. Stick cross-stitch plaque to centre of cake. Do trellis work and position wings. Pipe a shell around the base of the cake with a No43 tube and a rope following the shell with a No2.

Antique lace cake. This delicate cake could be made in any colour for an anniversary or birthday. The real lace around the base could be kept as a momento. The piping takes 12-15 hours so do it over several days.

To cover the cake, colour sugarpaste with jade green, or blue with a touch of green. A very pale colour is needed because of the daintiness of the work. Place cake on thick glass base with a bevelled edge, if wished, or on a cake board.

Pipe a shell around base with a No2 tube. Use a No00 tube with base colour icing to stick centre piece in position. Place lace around outer edge at different angles. Pipe small forget-me-nots on side. Place real lace around base with ribbon; stick with a little icing.

Peacock cake. Cover an oval cake in pale blue sugarpaste and leave to dry for at least two days. Dust with blue and green petal dust for background. Paint grass on green background with food colouring. Make peacock. Attach dragonfly to edge with icing. Pipe a shell around the base and finish off with a blue velvet ribbon and a scalloped rope piped with a No2 tube.

Horse and carriage wedding cake. Cover a square cake in pale blue royal icing. Make horses and carriage according to directions. Stick two horses in position with icing, support until dry. Pipe lines between them. Repeat with remaining two horses. Place carriage in position with icing. Join horses to carriage with two lines of icing. Dry completely. Make four runout collars from template, let dry. Attach collars. Pipe petit point lace in dark blue and stick in place. Pipe lines inside collars, a shell around base and a running line inside piped line.

Buttercream filigree on a chocolate cake. Cover an 18cm (7in) square cake with two coats of melted chocolate. Use a comb scraper on the sides. Leave to set. Make a pattern of grease-proof (waxed) paper from the template. Use a scriber or hat pin to transfer the pattern onto the top of the cake. Use green and peach buttercream, each with a No2 tube, to pipe the design. Sides and edges are piped freehand. Do not store cake in the refrigerator as the chocolate will form beads of moisture and the buttercream will separate.

Peach and chocolate gâteau. Cover a sponge gâteau base with peach buttercream. Use a comb scraper to decorate the surface. Divide the top into 16 portions with a long knife or gateau divider. Pipe a chocolate filigree heart for the centre decoration and 16 filigree pieces. Leave to set. Pipe a freehand S-scroll design on top and a shell round top and bottom edges with a No44 tube. Place heart and filigree pieces in position on the cake. Use a darker shade of peach to pipe the centre of the flowers with a No2 tube. Pipe additional decoration onto gâteau as shown.

Buttercream gâteau with chocolate centrepiece. The filigree pieces can be made in advance but assemble them shortly before use, as this decoration is difficult to store. Cover gâteau with natural coloured buttercream. Use a comb scraper on the top and round the side. Pipe top and bottom shells with a No44 tube; overpipe with No3, then overpipe again. Melt some milk chocolate; thicken with a little glycerine. Pipe four pieces of the design onto greaseproof or waxed paper. For the disc, run out a sheet of chocolate on greaseproof paper in a baking tin. Cut out a round plaque. Leave to dry. Stick plaque to the gâteau as shown and position filigree pieces. Pipe bulbs of buttercream on the top for contrast.

Easter egg. Mould a medium-sized chocolate egg. With pink chocolate pipe the water lily petals and dragonfly onto the polished outer side of the mould. Pipe some separate pink petals over a curved surface. Pipe pink chocolate lace onto waxed paper. Pipe yellow chocolate stamens and a green chocolate leaf. Stick onto egg along with the dragonfly. Stick additional petals onto lily at an angle. Pipe a small line of chocolate and stick lace around edge. Pipe green chocolate cornelli work on the board before or after lace has been attached. Stick a ribbon around the board and tie a bow in front of the egg.

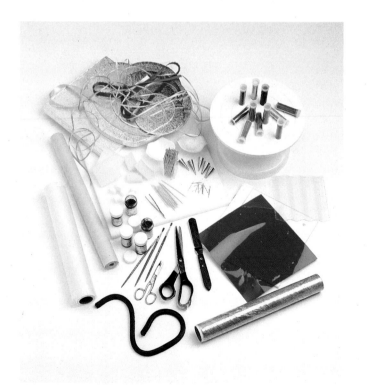